SELLING

DOMINATION

Rodney Hughes

Author | Entrepreneur | Sales & Marketing Expert

Published in the United States of America by

MarketingSS.

Selling Domination

ISBN 978-0-692-35321-9

Cover illustration by: Rodney Hughes

Rodney Hughes books are available at special discounts

when purchased in bulk for premiums and sales

promotions as well as for fund-raising or educational use.

Special editions or book excerpts can also be created to

specifications. For details, contact Rodney Hughes at

www.RodneyHughes.com

Manufactured in the United States of America

First printed January 2015

I dedicate this book to God, Tamara Hughes, Velma Hughes, Rodney Hughes Sr., Bianca Hughes, Marvine Ward, Oscar Ward, Kenneth Ward, all of my family, friends, and anyone who has ever believed in me.

FREE SALES MAXIMIZER CONSULTATION

Would you like me to personally double, triple, or even quadruple your business... For FREE?

Dear Success-Minded Friend,

I've set aside some time to talk to you, personally. During this time, I'll evaluate your business and work with you in a collaborative fashion to create a master plan (that you can implement immediately) to increase your sales and profitability.

There is absolutely no charge for this service, and there is absolutely no catch! If you enjoy our conversation and feel like you've gotten great value from it, then we can discuss what it would look like for us to work together long term. (There is no obligation, on your part, to work with me)

Here's the cool part

If you feel like I've wasted your time in our conversation (which this has never happened in over 10 years), I'll send you a check for $25 as compensation. No matter how you look at it, you will come out ahead!

If you would like to set up your complementary meeting with Rodney, please go to www.RodneyHughes.com and sign up, or call Rodney directly at 770-847-6611

Contents

Contents

10 Principles of Selling Domination

1. You're only in one business… You're in the money getting business. Never forget that!

2. You must establish a clear, concise, and compelling vision of your desired outcome. Then… only focus on completing one major step at a time.

3. Become sold on who you are, the value you bring, and your vision. (Become Certain)

4. Exercise full responsibility for the outcomes in your life (Mark of a true leader)

5. Never pre-judge someone's purchasing power or attempt to make a purchasing decision for your prospect. Treat each prospect like they're the most important and wealthy person in the world.

6. Ruthlessly prioritize your time! (Time is a gazillion times more valuable than any other resource you have available to you, outside of God!)

7. Beware of the Devil! Establish, nurture, and constantly grow your pipeline.

8. GSD (Get Stuff Done) with purpose. Always TMA (Test, Measure, and Adjust) until you get it right.

9. Always remember the #1 rule of selling… Seek alignment!

10. When closing a deal… Less is always more!

Introduction

When Geoff Nicholson, Spencer Silver and Arthur Fry invented the Post-It Note, few people understood its potential value—including their own bosses. The inventors' managers at paper company 3M didn't see the value in a little square that could be stuck to any surface and peeled off without leaving a residue, and as a result, they were getting nowhere with their product. But Nicholson believed in his idea. He had sample Post-it Notes made and handed them out to his co-workers. The notes were an immediate hit. Every time a colleague requested more, Nicholson would forward the request to his obtuse managers. Finally, the leaders of the commercial tape division were persuaded that that product could be a hit, and they started offering free samples in an Idaho test market. Almost everyone who tried the notes loved them—and the result was a famous product success story. [source: http://www.cbsnews.com/news/how-to-champion-an-idea-tips-from-the-invention-of-the-post-it-note/]

Today Post-It Notes are ubiquitous in offices, workplaces and college campuses, and their inventors are very rich men. But it wouldn't have happened if Nicholson and his co-inventors hadn't seen a need, believed in their product, and been incredibly persistent. As a result, they were able to dominate their marketplace. If you want to dominate your market, you need to emulate the traits that helped them succeed. In this book, you'll find out how.

Why should you care about learning how to dominate your sales environment? The answer to that question is simple: FINANCIAL SECURITY! Having the ability to dominate your market by effectively selling others on your ideas, products, and services has always been and will always be the most valuable skill that any person can ever acquire in business and in life. Think about it. It doesn't matter how great your ideas, products, or services are… If you can't sell others on your vision, at a price point that is high enough to generate an actual profit that is over and above your expenses, then no real value has been exchanged. Post-Its would have been useless if no one had ever had a chance to try them. It's only through the exchange of profitable value (SELLING) that you can position yourself to dominate in a marketplace. It's only through dominating in a marketplace that you can experience true security in your financial future.

In today's world, dominating the marketplace has only gotten harder—but it's also gotten even more important. Back in 2008, the entire world experienced the worst economic contraction since the Great Depression. Since 2008, not only has the economic landscape changed, but also the overall decline in trust from the marketplace has made it far more difficult to win in business. As entrepreneurs, managers, and sales professionals across the world strive to capture market share in these difficult economic times, only those who learn the art and science behind dominating a sales environment (*not* just competing in a sales environment) will enjoy the luxury of feeling SECURE in their economic future. When you compete in your market, you're just one of many businesses struggling to stay afloat. When you dominate, you're the top business in your market—the first choice people think of when making a buying decision, and a main authority on your product. Achieve that status, and it's easy to keep increasing your revenue.

By the end of this book, I intend on you having a clear understanding of the steps you can take immediately to start dominating your market. The skills and techniques that I'm going to share with you are pretty simple and very practical, but once you APPLY them to your business, you'll be able to open doors of opportunity that you never thought were within reach. You'll be able to truly take control of your life, start working with more of your ideal clients and enjoy the pleasure of not having to worry about where your next dollar is coming from. You'll be able to operate a system that will allow your business to work for you as opposed to you working for it!

CHAPTER 1

The 4 Pillars of Dominating Your Marketplace

Imagine you're shopping for computers online, and you see a brand of laptop you've never heard of before. The computer offers the RAM, screen resolution and other features that you're looking for, and it's priced a little cheaper than equivalent laptops from other brands. Would you buy it? If you're like most of us, probably not. You're making a big purchase, and you're willing to pay a little more for the security of getting a trusted brand, like HP or Dell. Or maybe you're already a brand loyalist and you know you're looking for, say, a Mac. These brands offer known features and quality control. Any new computer company will have to work hard to overcome this bias in favor of the familiar. If you're like most companies, your product is probably in the same position. And if you want to achieve market dominance, there's one big question you need to answer.

The question is simple… What must a company do to dominate their market? I believe that there are four key areas that must be focused on and developed for you to be able to position yourself, your product or your company as the dominant force in your market.

O—Overcome obscurity

P—Product

P—People

O—Operations

Let's take a look at each one of these pillars so you can have a better understanding of why they are so important.

OVERCOMING OBSCURITY

Obscurity is the number one challenge to having success in business. It's frustrating when you've worked hard to create something valuable and it fails, not due to lack of quality, but because your target customer doesn't know enough about it. That's obscurity, and that's where every successful product—including Apple, Nike and Heinz Ketchup—had to start. But within this designation, there are more complexities. There are three different levels of obscurity that must be addressed if you plan to successfully overcome this challenge and rise to market domination.

Level 1 Obscurity: **People don't know you exist.**

I'm willing to bet my last dollar that not everyone in your market that could potentially benefit from your product or service is aware that you even exist. That's true whether you're based in New York City and have to contend with thousands of competitors, or whether you're based in Mayberry, USA and count your potential customers in the thousands. Most people simply aren't very observant or invested in exploring all their options. This poses a very basic barrier to sales— if your potential customers do not know that you exist, good luck trying to sell them something. Your very first goal for overcoming obscurity is making a large percentage of people (in your market) aware of you, your company, and what you offer.

Level 2 Obscurity: **People don't know your value.**

I can't tell you how many times I've been introduced to a company, via some form of advertising, and couldn't clearly understand the value of that company. I'm sure we've all experienced this before. You get a flyer that's just a pretty stock photo with a company name and some contact information—basically, a glorified business card. Or you listen to a commercial, hear the jingle and snappy slogan, and still don't know what they sell. Or you spot a billboard in a plum location with a hilarious stock photo of a grumpy baby or cute animal, but no actual information. You now know this company exists, but you don't know what's special about them—or why you should give them your hard-earned money!

I've seen this kind of advertising hundreds of times. I won't name and shame the companies responsible—I couldn't even if I wanted to, since I don't remember who they are! There is a persistent myth that getting your name out there is enough to draw in customers. It's not. This is a surefire way to miss out on tons of sales. To make a purchasing decision, people need to know who your are, what you offer, and why it's valuable. Your customers are overloaded with marketers who constantly lie and overpromise, so if you're going to stand out, you need to find a creative way to give value as soon as possible. Make it simple for people to understand how valuable your products or services are up front. Always lead with value!

Level 3 Obscurity: **People aren't constantly thinking about you.**

I'd guess that in life, most of the ads we see are for things we've already heard of. On the surface, it might seem irrational for McDonald's to spend millions of dollars a year to remind us that they still serve hamburgers, or for Coke to let us know that their drink is brown and fizzy. We're even exposed to ads telling us that beef is "what's for dinner" and cotton is "the fabric of our lives." Have you ever wondered why companies spend so much telling us what we already know? They do it for one reason and one reason only… they want to stay on the top level of the consumer's mind!

It's not an accident that you have to consider McDonald's every time you think about a burger. It's not an accident that you have to consider Wal-Mart when you need household items. Even if you don't like these companies personally, you still have no choice but to at least consider them when you're thinking about what they offer. If you're going to dominate your market, you must find creative ways to stay on your prospect's minds. If your customers and prospects are constantly thinking about you, this dramatically increases the likelihood of your products and services being purchased. Buyers hate thinking, and want to deal with people and companies that they know, like and trust. Constantly stay in front of them and it will make their decision to do business with you ten times easier.

Each level of obscurity can be overcome. But to target your efforts most successfully, you have to know which one you're at. Focusing your time, energy, and resources on overcoming these three levels of obscurity—in the right order—can singlehandedly explode the amount of business that you're doing. Many companies get stuck at one of the obscurity stages because they're trapped in a myth like "just get your name out there." When taking action to overcome obscurity, you will need to have the right type of mindset. You mindset should be that of seeking omnipresence in your marketplace. "Omnipresent" is defined as "widely or constantly encountered; common or widespread." To ensure that your customer experiences your brand this way, you have to think about marketing from their perspective, not yours. You should think first about letting as many potential customers as possible know your value, then about establishing yourself as the default option in that category. Having a committed and consistent mindset of seeking omnipresence in your marketplace will help you focus on the right marketing ideas that will get you to the fastest path to the most cash.

So, how do you do that? If you're still struggling with Phase 1 obscurity, use cold calling and word of mouth to ensure that the most desirable potential clients in your market hear about you. Offering your current clients discounts or other benefits for referring new clients is a low-budget way to get your name out. Create a professional-looking website, and hire an SEO expert to make sure that it actually appears in searches by people who are interested in your product. Create accounts on the main social media networks so people can find you there.

Maybe you're already doing all this. If so, it's time to focus on the next step: Making sure your advertising and other public messaging conveys the message you want it to. An ad in the free weekly that's just a photo of your storefront? A website that appears well in search rankings, but conveys no content beyond a phone number and a list of products? A Facebook page that no one ever posts on? None of these will persuade people of your value. When it comes to advertising, focus on your customers' interests and create an ad that briefly and memorably conveys how you'll fulfill those interests.

For example, if you run a Turkish restaurant, your clients are looking for great service and a unique, exotic dining experience—quotes from satisfied customers may get that across. Maybe you run an electronic records service focusing on a specific medical specialty—you need to let your clients know that your product is tailored specifically to what they do. If you offer cloud storage to businesses, your customers are managers who don't want to hear a lot of technical jargon—you should emphasize that you'll solve their problems and provide quick, hassle-free setup.

If your website is bare-bones, maybe now is the time to add value to it by adding blog posts, short articles or informative Q&As that will keep visitors reading longer. And if you're making cold calls or talking to clients one-on-one, every part of the conversation after the introductory phase should focus on demonstrating value. In a later chapter, we'll focus on just how to achieve that. But there's one thing all these tactics have in common—they need to show that you believe in your product.

PRODUCT

Every company needs to sell something. What is your product? How in demand is your product? What's the real quality or perceived quality of your product? Is it easy for your target market to readily understand the value of your product? If possible, you should answer all these questions before selecting a product to represent and bring to market. And if your product is already established, you need to make sure you can communicate these answers to your customers.

You can be the best salesperson in the world, but if you're trying to sell a product that there is no demand for, you're spinning your wheels! When I consider working with a coaching client, I typically start by getting a firm understanding of the product that this particular coaching client is selling, and I try to determine how much demand there is for the product they're offering. If you're selling fried chicken, there's a fairly consistent demand; by contrast, a new product like Post-It Notes had no market until the inventors created one for it. Having a product that doesn't satisfy the needs, wants, or desires of the marketplace is a surefire way to go out of business fast. If you want to dominate your market and sell at a high level, you need to start by making sure that you're representing a product that you believe in, and a product that the market actually wants!

PEOPLE

Of course, there's more to success than just peddling what people already like. The story of coconut water is one example. In 2004, almost no Americans had heard of the drink. Then a pair of entrepreneurs, Michael Kirban and Ira Liran, got the idea of selling the Brazilian beverage to New Yorkers under the brand name Vita Coco. Since they were starting from scratch, the pair had to persuade stores to stock their product one by one. They did this by hiring a salesman who had a way with bodega owners. As the *New York Times* reports, "[the salesman] and his team memorized phrases in Spanish, Arabic, Korean and Hebrew and quickly learned to tailor their pitches to different ethnicities," haggling with Middle Eastern store owners, for instance. And they wooed customers with health claims and tons of free samples. When the drink got popular enough in independent stores, it was picked up by chains like Whole Foods. [http://www.nytimes.com/2014/07/27/business/for-coconut-waters-a-street-fight-for-shelf-space.html]

Coconut water is now a trendy and wildly popular post-workout drink, but it didn't sell itself—charismatic salespeople opened the door by a combination of persuasion, advertising and elbow grease. Could you do the same thing? Whether you're an entrepreneur, manager, or sales professional, how skilled are you and your people at the art and science of selling?   This is an important question!

In the past, I've been asked if I think that talented salespeople are made or born. For a very long time, I wasn't sure how to answer this question. After ten plus years of working with sales professionals along many different industries, I now have a very strong opinion on this question. My answer is: They're made.

That's right, talented sales professionals are made. I've seen many people in this profession who have dynamic personalities, and they can't sell to save their life! All of the heavy hitters I've met in this profession have worked very hard to learn what it takes to get people to say "yes." There really is a science and art to selling, and if you commit yourself to learning both sides, then you can dominate in your market. If you're going to dominate in your market, you must commit to learning everything you can about selling. The owners of Vita Coco could have had the best slogan and packaging in the world, but if they hadn't been able to relate to and charm small business owners, their business would have gone nowhere. If you can't sell effectively, it doesn't matter how good you become at marketing, you're going to screw up tons of opportunities and lose a lot of potential money.

OPERATIONS

Have you ever shopped around for an item online, picked the right one, and actually placed it in your shopping cart...only to abandon the sale because the buying process was just too much of a hassle? Maybe the website was full of glitches, kept timing out before you could complete the purchase, or demanded too much information from you to create an account before you could even view your shopping cart. When that happens, it's easier to complete the purchase elsewhere. There are many ways simple mistakes can sabotage a sure thing. This shows why operations are crucial to dominating your market. Chances are, you know this as a customer; you must keep it in mind as a seller too.

An easy way to lose a lot of money in business is to become really good at both sales and marketing, but have a poor operating system in place that ends up pissing off your clients or causing them to experience buyer's remorse. Operations are the logistical aspects of your business—your website, payment portal, shipping and handling system, supply network, etc. Your operating system ensures that your great product not only exists in theory but gets into the hands of people who want it, when they want it. If it doesn't, you not only upset your clients but lose tons of profit.

Dominating your market becomes very easy once you have the right operating systems in place. That's because the gap between finding out about a great product and actually experiencing it will be short and trouble-free. Your sales will start to generate at a high level once the infrastructure can support your dominating sales activities.

To make sure your operations aren't holding you back, seek out feedback from customers on the best and worst aspects of the buying process. If any aspect of it is slow and inconvenient, whether it's scheduling a consultation, placing an order or waiting for shipment, put a plan in place to fix it. Another tactic is to test your business's customer service from the client's perspective by visiting the website, or physical store, and trying to complete a purchase. Make notes on what you find and note any ways the experience could be made more convenient. Either way, make sure your operation not only can handle your current volume of business but is prepared for an increase in business.

Incredible customer service is one way businesses win over customers. But as we'll see in the next chapter, committing to incredible levels of effort in all levels of your business is key to achieving market domination.

CHAPTER 2

Go Incredible or Go Home!

People always ask me, "Rodney, what's the fastest way you know to grow a business?" Every time I'm asked this question, I know the person asking is probably not going to like my answer. Why? Because most people are looking for some type of magic formula that will relieve them of personal responsibility. They're hoping for some clever solution like posting just the right kind of content on the right social media network, or using some special formula to determine the "next big thing" in their field. All these tactics are too complicated. My answer to this question in simple: Take incredible amounts of action on a consistent basis in a consistent direction until the desired outcome is attained. This answer may disappoint some people, but it has two things in its favor: It's true. And it can change your life relatively fast.

When I say "incredible amounts of action," I'm not telling you to just take action for action's sake. Your goal should be to take incredible amounts of action on activities that will actually move your business forward as fast as possible. For instance… If you're used to contacting ten business owners per week to grow your corporate business, you may focus on contacting 50 business owners instead. If you currently make 40 prospecting calls per day, you should focus on making 80 prospecting calls instead. Of course, that's if these calls are working to get you more business in the first place. If they're not, you should devote some time to understanding what's not working. Are your calls failing because you're focusing on your needs and perspective as a business, instead of what value you can offer to others? Are you directing your prospective clients to a website that's confusing, unprofessional, or hard to contact you on? If that's the case, devote your energy to fixing the problem, and then go back to sales calls. I assure you, this instant surge of effort will help you uncover more opportunities and will lead to you generating more business immediately.

The easiest way I know to win in business and dominate your market is to operate at action levels that are so incredible that people start to look at you like a mad-person. This type of activity gives you an immediate advantage in your marketplace because most people are either taking average amounts of action or no action at all. Most of your direct competitors are stuck in a habitual routine that either causes them to win consistently, become stagnant, or lose in business. If you're willing to kick your activity up to incredible levels of action in the right areas of your business, then you will start to reach more people, create more opportunities, close more deals, and piss off a lot of your competitors. Operate at this level long enough, and your competition will cease to exist. Past competitors will then become admirers.

So, how do you operate at such a high energy level without burning out? The trick is to devote energy to the areas that will actually bring results. The first step to achieving this is to perform an analysis. Where did your current customers come from? Of your most lucrative clients, how did they find out about you? If a selling tactic (an ad, a cold call script) doesn't work, does your rate of success improve when you change it? Create a spreadsheet to track these factors. Too often businesspeople go through the motions of selling. But, because they get mediocre results, they're never motivated to ramp up their efforts. Once you put the effort into figuring out what works, positive reinforcement will motivate you to keep pouring energy into doing it.

I can vividly remember when I was hitting a particular rough patch in sales a few years ago. It just seemed like I was spinning my wheels, but I wasn't making any progress. It dawned on me that I was investing too much effort into too many areas that weren't giving me a positive ROI. I decided to focus primarily on the 20% of the activities that were giving me 80% of the results (This is known as the Pareto Principle). I decided that I would focus on taking massive amounts of action in these areas and neglect the other things that were distracting me. What were the results of taking this type of action? In less than a month, I was able to more than triple my sales! The month prior I generated approximately $20,000 in revenue, and the following month, I was able to generate over $65,000 in revenue. Not bad right! As I began that new month with this new laser type focus, fear no longer was a problem of mine. I became naturally motivated to perform as I started seeing the results that I was achieving. [Example from your/your clients' experience would be great here]

So, what determines whether a selling tactic—whether it's advertising, cold calling, a website, an in-person pitch, or even a storefront—will be successful? Of course, trial and error plays a role in determining what works for you. But there's one thing that all successful tactics have in common. In the next chapter, we'll see what that is.

CHAPTER 3

Understand this Concept, and Selling Will Become a Breeze!

If I could write a guide to sales in only one sentence, it would be this: PROSPECTS ONLY CARE ABOUT THEMSELVES! Drill this concept into your mind until you fully understand it. While this may sound a little extreme to some people, I assure you, this is a factual statement when it comes to the selling environment. When your prospect woke up this morning, I promise you, he or she did not think about anything that you want, need, or desire. They're not worried about whether you were feeling especially creative when you sketched out your new line of ski boots, or whether you're annoyed by your customers' cluelessness about cyber security, or whether your heart swells with pride when you look at your rental company's fleet of limousines. The only things that were on their mind were the things that THEY want, need, or desire. That might be a trendy ski boot that will arrive before they leave on that ski weekend, a managed security service that solves all their computer problems for a flat rate, or a limo service that will make their daughter feel like a VIP on prom night.

This is a very simple, powerful concept; yet so many sales professionals seem to forget this concept or flat out don't acknowledge it. Have you ever seen a website that was full of glowing stories about the business owner's amazing achievements and business philosophy, but didn't make it easy to find out where to buy their products, how much they cost, or even what their storefront hours were? Ever walked into a store selling guitars or computers and been treated to a long, technical spiel about the salesperson's favorite model—one that may have demonstrated their incredible technical knowledge, but went way over your head? Or how about that email from a job-seeker that didn't make clear, in the first paragraph, what they're good at and why you should read their *résumé*?

In all these cases, you probably lost interest fast because your needs weren't being addressed. Understanding this concept will allow you to position your communication (with your prospect) in such a way that the prospect will literally feel drawn towards doing business with you because they will feel like you understand them so well!

When I train my clients on selling, I always start by painting this picture for them: "Imagine that you work for ABC Car Company, and this mobster told you that they would kill you if you didn't sell a car to this guy named Adam. Before Adam came to the car lot, the mobster tells you that Adam has been diagnosed as having extreme narcissism. Equipped with this information, how would you go about selling Adam a car so you can save your life?" This hypothetical situation sounds pretty extreme. But in practice, it's not so crazy—it captures the reality of the way selling works. Forget about your ego and personal priorities, appeal to Adam's narcissistic nature, and you can achieve the ultimate result of selling him a car.

So, how does this work in practice? First, you need to research your clients. Who are they, what are their budgets and priorities, where does your product fit into their lives? Is this a new type of product for them, or are they switching brands? Is your product a luxury or a necessity to them? What other brands might they be tempted by? Create a document describing your client's demographics and attitudes in as much detail as you can.

Next, research your client's thoughts and feelings by seeking out feedback. You can do that through feedback forms or surveys from your own customers, or by seeking out opinions about your type of product online, in forums and review sites like Yelp. What do customers seem most impressed by? What do they describe themselves most as looking for? What do they complain about the most? Doing this type of research may open your eyes to aspects of your business you never considered before. For instance, say your run a cyber security business. From your perspective, if you protect your clients from getting hacked or having their IP stolen, you've succeeded. From the client's perspective, all that stuff is pretty abstract. They may place more value on customer service and communication skills. If you can't explain to the tech-illiterate management why they need to pay for that VPN or new modem, they might feel they're getting ripped off—no matter how big a bargain you're offering.

Your service is only as valuable as your client thinks it is. If more entrepreneurs, managers, and sales professionals would embrace this type of mindset, I'm sure they would find selling to be a much easier act than it previously was. Focus solely on your clients and helping them find what they want and they will typically respond by giving you their money!

Of course, when you first start communicating with a client, you can't just blurt out a laundry list of details about your prices, products and customer service —no matter how great they are. You need to present each piece of information when your customer is curious, primed, and ready to hear it. In the next chapter, you'll learn how to do just that, creating a selling process that maximizes your chances of making the sale.

CHAPTER 4

5 Steps You Must Learn to Become a Master at Selling

Appealintg to your client's wants and needs will allow you to attract tons of people to you, who are predisposed to buy the product you're selling. That's great! But you can't dominate your market with hypothetical buyers. To succeed in business, you have to close the deal. Imagine you work for that car dealership, and you've attracted a potential buyer with the offer of an "everything must go" sale. She's ready to buy a car, she has the funds, and you have her desired make and model in stock. None of that matters if you can't persuade her that you're giving her your best possible deal, and that this purchase is the smartest choice she could possibly make. Bad salesmanship can drive great prospects away. Let's make sure that you have a firm understanding of the selling process so you can easily convert these predisposed leads into paying customers.

There are many different types of selling situations I can cover to help you understand this process, but I'm going to focus on the most difficult of them all… cold calling! If you can understand and become effective at conducting cold calls, you'll easily be able to win in the other types of selling situations. In order to master a pure cold calling situation, you must first start by understanding the five main steps in the sales process:

5 Steps to Making the Sale:

• Get attention

- Establish interest
- Align/build value
- Gain commitment
- Coordinate/reaffirm

We all know that first impressions are lasting impressions. Mastering the first two steps of the sales process will allow you to quickly determine if a prospect is worth your time. Jumping ahead to building value won't work if you haven't laid that groundwork. Gerry Robert, an extremely successful publishing expert, Owner of Black Card Books, and author of *Multiply Your Business*, summed it up perfectly when he wrote that "Selling is like kissing. You can't kiss someone who is backing away from you. The best kissers are always leaning forward. That's what you need to get prospects doing… leaning forward toward you. (Not trying to sell people who are backing away from you—like so many people do)" (21). Trying to sell to a reluctant buyer is an uncomfortable process—and it's a waste of time. If your goal is to dominate your market, your most valuable commodity in doing so is your time. Every sale demands an investment of time—you must make sure it's not used pitching to buyers who aren't really interested. Becoming great at the first two steps will allow you to prioritize your selling efforts.

GETTING ATTENTION

You may have the physical copy of *Selling Domination*, but let's imagine that you're viewing this book through the downloadable version. Chances are, you're reading this on your computer, and you have a web browser open with one or more active tabs. Within those tabs, how many advertising messages are open, trying to get your attention? Sidebar ads. Facebook ads and sponsored posts. Popup ads. At the bottom of every news article, there's a list of trashy but tempting articles with headlines like "Ugliest Celebrity Yearbook Photos."

And that's not even counting the actual retailer websites, all of them offering pretty pictures and special deals in the hopes that you'll stick around, browse and buy. From your customer's perspective, you're just one of many attention-hungry advertisers. In a day and time when prospects are constantly being bombarded with tons of marketing messages, you must learn how to break through the noise and gain attention for yourself.

There are literally hundreds, maybe even thousands, of ways that you can go about creatively gaining attention for yourself and your product, but they all have some things in common. They all start with getting attention and keep it by generating positive feelings about your product or service. So many people are petrified of performing cold calling efforts, but cold calling is no different in practice than any other kind of advertising. And if you're willing to become good at it, you have a huge advantage in your market place.

When performing a cold call, you should think of the process as split into two halves. The first two steps are the first half, and the last three steps are the second half. The goal of the first half is gaining exposure—communicating what you have to offer to the client, and persuading them of its value—and identifying potential opportunities. You do that by listening to the client, and learning about their goals and needs. When you've done that you'll be in a good position to make a sale. The goal of the second half is to align and fully close the deal.

So, how to get started? The opening phase of the process is a time to give and get information, but that doesn't mean you should start from scratch asking your potential client who they are and what they do. In order to give you an advantage in the first half, it's always best to start by doing some research on the company. Find out their history, specialty and strengths and weaknesses—how big are they? Who are they trying to sell to? What might be their priorities? And most importantly, research who will actually make the decision on whether to buy the item you're offering. Talk to anyone else, and there's a good chance you are wasting your time. If you can already have a name walking through the door, this will increase your odds of getting to that person quickly. If you do not have the name, you want to go in very nice and ask to speak with the person who would handle your type of inquiry (i.e. business owner, manager, etc). Then, clearly and decisively, you want to make it clear make your pitch to that decision maker who you are and why you want would like a piece of their time.

All this might sound obvious—and it is! It really is that simple. If you want to gain immediate attention for yourself, simply be willing to do what most people are unwilling to do. In this particular example, walking into the desired business and asking to speak with the person who is likely the decision maker will immediately gain the attention that you need to qualify for the opportunity. You'll probably be surprised to find out how reachable decision makers are. Sure, once in a while you'll hit a brick wall—but often you'll end up talking to someone with the authority to make that purchase *today*.

ESTABLISH INTEREST

Now you're ready to make your initial pitch. Your goal here is to be short, sweet, and to the point. You're dealing with the potential decision maker, and the number one thing on his or her mind is… "who is this person and what do they want?" The average prospect takes anywhere from four to ten seconds to make a decision in their mind about whether they're going to entertain you or not. This doesn't mean that they're making a purchasing decision during these first few seconds, but they are quickly determining if you are there to offer something valuable or to waste their time.

So, you should try to make that sale before they lose interest, right? Wrong. This part of the sales process is often times mishandled, and leads to many potential sales being lost. Prior to every call, it is important to have a very clear understanding of what your objective is for that call. If you're conducting a cold call, your primary objective should be to take that prospect from the cold call stage to the lukewarm stage. You should never enter into a cold call situation expecting to sell someone on your product. This is why so many salespeople experience so much rejection when it comes to cold calling. They're approaching the process from the wrong angle. Instead of looking to make a sale, focus on making the prospect aware of who you are, what you offer, and why your offer is something worth learning more about.

So, you're not actively selling during this stage. Here's the reality… You can be the best sales professional in the world, but if the prospect does not have a need, want, or desire for the product or service you're selling, you'll never be able to convince them to buy what you're selling. That's why this step is so vital! This step will allow you to quickly identify if this prospect is worth your time or not. As a rule of thumb, always remember this… *Never sell to someone unless they have clearly identified themselves as having interest in what you offer.* This will allow you to dramatically reduce the amount of rejection you will experience, save time, protect your ego, have more meaningful conversations, and make more money faster!

So, in this conversation, focus on giving all the information a person would need to understand your product, phrased in a way that's focused on their specific type of business. Imagine receiving a similar call at your place of business (or home), and make a list of the questions you'd want answered—then place those answers front and center in your conversation. Focus the conversation on answering the target's questions, not on asking questions about whether they will commit to a purchase.you want to focus on making sure that your prospect is somewhat predisposed to buy what you're selling. As an example, let's imagine that you own a group fitness training business and you want to build your corporate clientele. You decide that you want to host a free group training session this Saturday to help your corporate prospects see how great your training is and seedecide if they would like to join your program. You do some research and identify some potential prospects to call on. When you walk into your prospect's office, the conversation might sound like this:

You –: Hi there… Is John in today? (*Act like you're supposed to be there.*)
Receptionist –: Yes, was John expecting you today?
You –: He should be… Just tell him Adam is up front…. (*Create familiarity.*)
Receptionist –: Ok ay.
John –: Hi Adam, do we know each other?
You –: Perhaps (*quick pause*). I have a quick question for you… (*quick pause*)
You –: I own one of the top group fitness training businesses here in Atlanta (*Ppeople like dealing with winners*), and I'm hosting a free group training session this Saturday at 10 a.m. for business owners in this area… It's going to be tons of fun and a great workout. Does that sound like something you would be interested in attending?
John –: Sure… How do I sign up?

In this particular example, the remainder of the sales process would take place at the end of the actual group training session. Although this example is based on the fitness niche, this type of approach can work for any type of business. Sometimes you'll finish this step and immediately go into the alignment phase, and sometimes you'll need to schedule time at a later date. Remember, when you're cold calling, you're catching the prospect in the middle of them doing something that had their attention prior to you coming through the door. The primary focus of this approach is getting to the point and establishing commitment from the prospect that it is okay for us to move forward in the sales process, whether that's done immediately or at a later time that is more convenient for the prospect. That's it!

ALIGNMENT/BUILDING VALUE

Once you've completed the first two steps successfully, you can be confident that you're dealing with a person who is interested in learning more about what you're selling. But that does not mean that they're ready to make a purchasing decision. If you're getting strong, clear signals that the prospect is not interested—such as them failing to ask any questions, or telling you outright that they're not interested—you should graciously thank them for their time and end the conversation rather than wasting your time on more talk. If they are willing to move forward in the discussion keep talking, it's time for you to learn more and seek alignment. You must first start by finding out why your prospect was interested in speaking with you, and figuring out what's important to him or her. [Should salespeople schedule a second call or visit to make the sale? You state earlier that the first call should only focus on taking potential clients to the lukewarm stage, so I think you should discuss how they should progress to that second conversation.]

This step in the sales process is the part that most salespeople struggle with. They're bursting with great information and ready to deliver it to their target. But this step requires you to ask great questions and be a great listener. It's not enough to know *that* this prospect is interested in your offer—you must understand why. What **outcome** is your prospect ultimately trying to reach? Know that, and you can emphasize all the reasons your product or service will deliver that outcome. Too often salespeople focus on selling features and tools, before they fully understand the outcome that the prospect is trying to reach. Therefore, the salesperson is guessing about what is important to that prospect, and will likely sell features that are not important. This is an easy way to get your prospect to disengage with you as a salesperson.

Always remember this… The number one rule of selling is always seek alignment! Let me be clear… The number one rule of selling is to *seek* alignment, not force alignment! Forcing alignment is what con artists do to quickly build trust and faith. I do not want you to use this philosophy to con people out of their money. Only align with a prospect if you really believe that you can deliver the desired outcome. Going back to the example of cyber security, if a client wants round-the-clock phone service and a support team who can be on-site within an hour, and your service offers support with a 48-hour wait time, your client will be disappointed with the service— and tell others so. The fastest word-of-mouth advertising you can ever have is that of a pissed- off client who was lied to, and you don't want those types of problems. If you cannot deliver the desired outcome, then make sure that you inform the prospect. If you can deliver a partial outcome, then make sure that you manage that expectation effectively, and your prospect will trust you much faster.

To align, start by asking the right questions that help you understand the prospect's desired outcome first, and then structure your selling communication so that it aligns with the desired outcome(s) that your prospect has in mind. When you successfully communicate in this way, you will start to paint the picture in your prospect's head of success because you will be building value in their mind regarding your product. We've all been in the position of experiencing a problem or frustration ("the network goes down all the time, and nothing gets done while we wait for it to come back up") and feeling that no one is working to solve it. From your prospect's perspective, there is no greater feeling than to communicate with someone who understands what you're going through and offers sound advice on the next steps to take.

In this context, "maybe" won't cut it. When you're aligning your communication with your prospect's desired outcome, it is extremely important that you speak with certainty about the solution that you have to offer. You have to speak with certainty (as you align) so that your prospect will feel a sense of security about the decision they're making to do business with you. In a time of so much uncertainty in the world, you need to be that beacon of certainty in your prospect's life regarding this immediate decision.

Aligning and building value become easy once you understand this process. This is the step where great sales professionals shine. My dad was a successful businessman, and he used to always say "If you sell well enough, closing is a breeze!" For a long time, I didn't really understand what my dad was talking about, but now I totally understand. If you align properly and build enough value through your alignment, then your prospect will be eager to do business with you; all you have to do is just ask for the business. If you become really great at this step, then some of your prospects may tell you that they don't care how much it costs… "Sign me up!"

GAIN COMMITMENT

Gaining commitment from your prospect is, hands down, the most important step of the selling process! This is the step when you ask your prospect to make a decision about whether they're going to do business with you or not.   Now it's time to get a full commitment from this prospect. Now it's time for you to directly ask for the business! You might think that this is the easy part—but it's not.

Over the years, I have found it amazing to watch how good people can be at the first three steps, and then when it comes time to ask for the business, they either totally bomb it or they flat out don't ask for the business. IT STILL BLOWS MY MIND! I could write a whole book on this topic, but for the purpose of this book, I'm going to keep it short and sweet. No value (and I do mean NO VALUE) is exchanged if you do not get a commitment to do business. You may feel like it's obvious what you have in mind, and that it "goes without saying" you want to make a sale...but if you don't say it, you don't give your prospect a chance to say yes. It does not matter how much someone may need, want, or desire your help; if you do not ask them to do business with you, they won't. If you don't arrange to do business together then no value is exchanged. If no value is exchanged, then the prospect doesn't benefit from your time together and you don't benefit either! It just equates to a big waste of time!

The gaining commitment step is also known as closing the deal. There are so many salespeople who want to make more out of this step than what it actually is. Closing the deal isn't some magical dance, ritual, or spell where you have to say the magic words. All you're doing is asking for the business. That's it!

I believe that most entrepreneurs, managers, and sales professionals find this step difficult because they're either approaching the process the wrong way or they have some mental insecurity about asking people for money. If you're approaching the process of selling from the wrong angle, then this is an easy fix. Just start approaching the process as I outline it in this book. If you have some type of mental insecurity about asking people for their money in exchange for a valuable service, then here's my suggestion... You need stop trying to sell people on your product or service until you're 100% convinced that your product or service is worth the money that you're asking for.

I once worked for a company where I was selling a product that I did not believe in. At first I was selling well, but as my faith in the product started to wither, so did my sales. I ended up making the decision to take my selling service to another company where I ended up flourishing. In retrospect, I don't believe that I made the wrong decision to leave this company, but I do have a different perspective on that situation now that I've matured. The real problem that I was having was that I wasn't willing to ask for more money, and therefore my clients weren't receiving the benefits that they were looking for. I was pitching the cheaper, less effective version of the product because I wasn't willing to sell the "full-service" version. You see, now I realize that the problem actually wasn't the product itself, it was me. I had a deep insecurity about asking for large sums of money, and it ended up causing me to look for an excuse to not believe in the product. If I would have first completely sold myself on my product, and then executed the steps effectively, I would have had no problem asking for these large sums of money, and I would have succeeded in that position.

When you get to this step in the sales process, make sure that you keep things simple and direct. If you've executed the previous steps effectively, you should have no problem with this step. Just ask for the business, and SHUT UP! When asking for the business, excess talking is not your friend. You need to remain calm and confident, and ask the closing question as if you already know that they're going to say yes. And if you set the proper foundation, they will.

COORDINATE / REAFFIRM

Congratulations... You've closed the deal! But there is one more thing you need to do before moving on to your next prospect. You need to coordinate and reaffirm the deal that just got closed. This step is vital to your ultimate success in this sale. You need to understand that most people don't like making decisions. Think about your own past experience, and it's obvious why. Most people have been burnt in the past from a decision that they made that did not go well. Their biggest fear is making another bad decision that will cause them to lose money, feel stupid, and be judged negatively by their friends, family, or co-workers. Therefore, most people suffer from "decision constipation." They're too slow to decide, and when they do, they're likely to backtrack and give themselves more time to change their minds.

So, if you're successful in getting a person to make a purchasing decision and you want to avoid any type of buyers remorse, you don't want to wait and call them the next day or week—or even hour—to get payment information, arrange signatures, or schedule the installation. It is vitally important that you follow through on your promises by immediately coordinating the necessary next steps in the delivery process. And you need to reaffirm to this client how great a decision they just made. This is the time to leave the client feeling good by emphasizing how quickly the great effects of your service will take affect, how hassle-free it will be, and which of their problems or frustrations will disappear once your product is delivered.

Some types of sale will not require any kind of coordination—for instance, if all you need to do is ship a physical item to them. But if your type of sale does require you to do some form of coordination, you want to make sure that you over-deliver. When you break selling down to its simplest form, selling is just the act of making promises and delivering on those promises. If you do this well, you'll have a client that you can potentially generate thousands, even millions from over the life of your business relationship. If you've told them their service will be switched on by Thursday, ideally it should be on by Tuesday or Wednesday. If you've told them their internet speed will double, it should at least double—maybe even triple. This is why you must keep a pulse on how your product is being delivered and how the coordination process is moving along. If there are glitches in the process, you give time for doubt or buyer's remorse to sink in.

Some salespeople hang up the phone happy to have made a sale and don't trouble themselves with what happens next. That's a mistake. Unsatisfied clients create a bad reputation for your product that makes it harder to sell—and over time, disappointing people will make you less confident in what you're selling. One of the easiest ways to reduce buyer's remorse is to always focus on immediately reaffirming with your client that he or she made a great decision. This may seem really simple and possibly even unnecessary—after all, they just decided to buy your product!—but this will go a long way toward making sure your client is confident in choosing you. So how do you do that? You can simply summarize the key benefits your product offers to them, give a personal anecdote of why you personally use this product, quote an existing client who told you why they're happy with the product, or mention an exciting perk (like free gift with purchase or exclusive member benefits) that you hadn't mentioned before. There are many different ways to go about doing this, so don't be afraid to get creative—what counts is that you really mean it, and want them to feel happy about the decision they just made.

So, what have we seen in this chapter? You started by bursting through the noise and gaining the prospect's attention, then you established that he or she was interested in learning more about what you have to offer. You then found out what was important to your prospect and made sure that you aligned your communication and built value so that the prospect became excited and eager to do business with you. You asked for the business, got it, and made sure that you reaffirmed their great decision and kept a pulse on the delivery process. You left them happy, feeling like a smart decision-maker, and excited to start getting the benefits of your product. That's selling the right way—not guilting or pressuring some hapless target into buying—showing them why doing business with you is a win for everyone.

CHAPTER 5

It Always Has Been, and Always Will Be a Numbers Game

In the last chapter we addressed all the touchy-feely stuff—how you make people feel good about you and your product. But selling is a numbers game... it always has been, and always will be. Why? Because you can be the world's greatest closer, but if you do not reach enough people, you will not be able to sell enough to make a living.

How you do that depends on where you work. Some companies have a marketing department that is tasked with reaching a large number of people who may be predisposed to buy what that company is selling. In this situation, you have a co-worker that is doing the footwork to find and deliver ready-to-buy prospects, and it is your responsibility to get them closed. This division of labor makes things a little easier. In other companies, you (business owner or sales professional) must proactively go out into the marketplace to find and close your deals. But regardless of how your company operates from a marketing perspective, the reality is still the same: You must contact a large number of people so you can uncover enough opportunities to hit the company profit goals. If you don't do this effectively, for a long enough period of time, then your company will cease to exist.

Of course, you know you need to contact potential clients. But there's more to the process than that. When it comes to dominating your market from a selling perspective, you want to focus on reach and frequency. Reach is the number of people that you're able to contact with your marketing efforts. Frequency is the number of times that a person comes in contact with your message. You want to reach a large number of people and make sure that they consistently come into contact with your marketing message. This is very important because you don't know who your clients are and what marketing activity will push them over the edge to finally decide to do business with you. People are not logical creatures...a buyer may be persuaded of all the reasons to buy your product, but simply be too lazy, indecisive or distracted to take action nine out of ten times they hear your message. This is why the concept of massive action is so important from a marketing perspective. It forces you to constantly focus on reaching more people and thinking of creative ways to show the same message.

But first, you have to get your foot in the door. Increasing the number of people that you contact with your message is by far the number one way that I know to go about increasing your sales. Increasing the number of people you contact is the one factor that you have 100% control over in the selling process. Think about it: Regardless of how good you are at the skill of selling, you can't force someone to want to buy your product. All you can focus on doing is contacting enough people who are interested in potentially buying what you have to offer. Once you've identified these people, then the skill of selling serves you well. This is why selling is a numbers game! You have to consistently find the people who are interested in what you have to offer, and then be skilled enough to close the deal. Contact a large sum of people, and uncover a large sum of opportunities, and you'll be well on your way to dominating your market.

The first step is to simply track how many people you're currently contacting, and set a manageable, but ambitious, goal for increasing that number. For instance, if you currently make 20 contacts a week, you could aim to increase it to 50—or even 100. How high you aim depends on the nature of your job and how much time you have to devote to making calls. If you work in an office setting, you may be able to find one non-essential task to cut. If you own your own business, you could aim to spend one extra hour per weekday making calls. Another factor to consider is avoiding wasted time on calls. You can do this by cordially ending calls if the prospect doesn't seem interested in what you have to say, and in making sure your callers are prepared to hear you out (not prepping for a big meeting or on their way out the door) before you begin a pitch. You can achieve this by asking a client "is this a badthis a good time to talk"—and if you hear a yes, or signs of uncertainty, arrange a time to call back later.

Once you've put your plan for increased volume into effect, track how many calls you actually succeed in making and whether you've reached your goal. If not, make a note of what you think is holding you back, and whether you can fix it. If so, consider raising your goal even higher. Ideally, you should keep increasing your volume of calls until you are on track to start meeting your long-term financial goals. In the next chapter we'll look in depth at how to do just that.

CHAPTER 6

Rainmakers Reverse Engineer Their Success. You Should Too!

"Easier said than done": That applies to a lot of things, including finishing a marathon, finding true love, and catching the world's biggest bass. And it definitely applies to the goal of dominating your market. Like most hard tasks, this goal has a psychological component. It involves a lot of work, but it also involves changes in thinking that business people aren't necessarily prepared for. The concept of selling domination is often a difficult concept for most entrepreneurs, managers, and sales professionals to wrap their heads around because their unconscious minds can't readily connect the dots. Your conscious mind may really like the idea of dominating your market, but if you do not create a strong realistic vision for accomplishing your goal, then your unconscious mind will start flooding your mind with doubt based on its current belief system. Because of this dynamic, you must first start by reverse engineering your success.

Reverse engineering your success forces you to establish a very clear vision of what future success looks like. In business, that vision might include number of stores, job title, brand prestige, or the type of lifestyle you live, but for now we'll focus on sales figures. Start with a sales goal that, if achieved, would place you at the top of your market. Once you have this number, you must then start by breaking it down into realistic numbers that are easy for you to wrap your head around. If I try to convince a business owner who is used to generating $100,000 worth of sales in a year that they can increase their business to $400,000 by the end of next year, I need to start by breaking down the $400,000 into a more workable goal. If I don't, there is a strong likelihood that this business owner will feel overwhelmed by the task of quadrupling his or her sales in such a short time frame, and will not be bought- in on the idea that this can actually be doable.

Here's an example of how I would go about breaking this huge number down into a more realistic goal:★

★ *example inspired by Bob Proctor*

1. Take $400K and divide it by 12, since there are 12 months in a year. ($33,333.33 per month)

2. That's a lot of money, so lets break it down even further… Let's divide $33,333.33 by 4.3 since there are 4.3 weeks in each month. ($7,751.94)

3. There is still a great chance that my prospect would consider this to be a lot of money, so lets break it down even further. Lets divide $7,751.94 by 2 ($3,875.97). This means that from Monday to Wednesday and from Thursday to Saturday you have to figure out how to generate $3,875.97.

4. Even this might seem like a very insurmountable figure to achieve, so let's break it down even more. Let's just divide $3,875.97 by a random number like 120. ($32.30)

Okay…. Now we have a number that we can work with! By choosing the random number 120, we can break that really huge $400K number down into a much more realistic number of $32.30. But what does this mean? This means that you do not have to figure out how to make $400K anymore. All you need to focus on is figuring out a way that you can convince 120 people from Monday to Wednesday to pay you $32.30, and then figure out how to do it again from Thursday to Saturday each week.

I'm sure you would agree that it is much easier to wrap your head around figuring out a solution to finding 120 people every 3 days to pay you $32.30 than it is to figure out how to magically generate $400K in one year. Once you've broken down the numbers into a realistic, attainable goal, you can now start to focus on strategies and tactics that will allow you to accomplish this realistic goal.

To put this plan into action, think about the current cost of your products and your current number of clients. If your goal is $32.30 and you sell widgets that cost $33, you need to persuade about 120 people every 3 days to buy one. That's 40 additional sales per day that you need to make, either by attracting new customers or persuading existing ones to make another purchase. Now you have a concrete idea of how much you need to amp up your selling efforts each day in order to meet your goal.

What if your products costsproducts cost more than $32.30? Then try breaking your original monthly figure down in a different way. For instance, let's say you sell a business-to-business subscription service that costs $1000 per month. You've already determined that your goal is an additional $33,333.33 income per month. To meet or exceed this goal in revenue from subscriptions, you would have to sell 34 new subscriptions over the course of a year (34 multiplied by 1000 = $34,000). Thirty-four subscriptions sold in a year averages out to .63 per week, or approximately one new sale every ten days. Now you just have to calculate how many calls or contacts you'd have to make to achieve one additional successful sales call every ten days. Do this, and you've exceeded your goal!

This is how winners make massive jumps in production. This is how you can become a Rainmaker in your market and create a plan for dominating your market!

CHAPTER 7

A Secret Weapon That Will Give You an UNFAIR Advantage in Selling

Take a second and think about the most successful people that you know, either in your direct market or in other industries. It seems like they have the golden touch. Money comes to them with ease. What makes these people so successful? What is the secret weapon that allows them to completely dominate their field? The answer is simple: Aauthority. These aren't just people who happen to have a job, a title, or even a special talent. They've done a great job of creating and positioning themselves as an authority in their marketplace. People around them believe they know more about their given field than almost anyone else, and new contacts can also sense this greater knowledge and judgment. How do they achieve this? Authority is twofold. It comes from actually knowing a lot, and from being able to communicate that knowledge to others—without relying on reciting facts or boring lectures. Authority allows the greater-than-life people in your life to easily establish and take over markets, and it can do the same thing for you.

You've probably noticed the effects of authority in your own reactions. If a salesperson sounds uncertain, you lose interest. If a new business contact radiates lack of confidence, you won't go to them when you need input on a tricky question. And if a business website is amateurish or unprofessionally designed, you won't be willing to spend big money in their online store. We don't give confidence to those who don't act like they deserve it.

Science backs up this effect, too. In 1963, Dr. Stanley Milgram published a study in the *Journal of Abnormal and Social Psychology* (later expanded into a book). Milgram believed that if a person is viewed as having a high enough level of authority, they could easily get people to do just about anything they asked. His team tested this idea with a tricky two-layered experiment. They recruited student subjects who thought they were testing the effects of punishment on learning. A pair of students would enter the lab, where one would be assigned the role of "teacher" and the other the role of "learner." The "learner" would then be led into a neighboring room and be hooked up to electrodes (or so it appeared). The learner was tasked with memorizing word pairs. If the student gave the wrong responses, Dr. Milgram would ask the "teacher" to flip a switch and administer an electrical shock. If that wasn't enough... every time the student answered the question incorrectly, the wattage would be increased and the other student would still be asked to flip the switch.

The findings from this experiment were fascinating. At first, the "teachers" felt a little hesitant to flip the switch, but reluctantly followed the orders of the doctor. After about five incorrect answers, the student that was flipping the switch started to hear the person in the other room start to scream, yet in almost every case, the student continued to follow the command of the doctor. After a couple more wrong answers, the screams that were coming from the other room started to sound like he was dying! Nonetheless, almost every student remained obedient to the commands of the Doctor to flip the switch.

Thankfully, this was just an experiment—the screams were faked, and no real electrical shocks were used. The purpose of this experiment was to see just how far someone could be persuaded to inflict pain on another when being told to do so from an authority figure. When they asked the student, who was flipping the switch, why they continued to flip the switch even though they knew they were clearly inflicting pain to another and could possibly kill them, the response was interesting. The student said that he continued because the guy giving the orders was a doctor, so he just did what he was told to do.

Scary? Absolutely. The significance of this story is how easily people can be influenced to take action when the suggestion is coming from someone in authority. Note that it's not "real" authority—a doctor or lawyer's hard-won knowledge—that produces this effect. Rather, it's the trappings of authority, like a doctor's lab coat, stethoscope, and air of confidence. Dr. Milgram and his associates acted like they expected obedience. If they had sounded tentative or uncertain, the students would likely have listened to their own uncertainty and left the experiment. Authority needn't be used for sinister purposes. Just like many things in life, this power can be used for good or evil. There are many cases in the business world where a person wants to make a big decision, knows it could benefit or even transform their business, but doesn't want to act because they feel fearful. As we discussed earlier, people fear making a foolish decision, so they delay and procrastinate—even if their failure to act harms them. This is where an authority figure can benefit them. By telling them that your new cloud storage system is what they need to keep their data secure, or that your newsletter will protect them from lawsuits, you reassure that that it's okay to act.

For the purpose of what I'm trying to teach you in this book about selling domination, I would suggest that you always strive to position yourself as an authority figure in your market, but make sure that your ultimate goal in doing so is to add value to the lives of others. There are major consequences that await people who abuse their position of authority, so it is always best to do what is right by people.

Here's another example, showing the good side of authority. At the time of writing this book, I'm recovering from ankle surgery. I broke my ankle playing kickball (Yes… grown men and women play kickball, but that is a subject for an entirely different book!), and I went to my doctor's office hoping that I did not have to have surgery. My doctor (who's a specialist in orthopedic surgery) told me that I did need an operation, and he showed my why it was important. Without second-guessing (because he's an authority and because I believed that he had my best interest in mind), I decided to commit to his treatment plan, which ultimately cost me over $30,000. I bring this situation up for one reason: His authority on this subject made it very easy to take his advice and commit to a high-ticket offer. By the way... It took less than 15 minutes for me to be convinced that this was the right solution for me. If I did not view him as an authority on this subject, I likely would not have done business with him and if I did, he would have had a lot of convincing to do. Again, it wasn't logical arguments or a large volume of facts that convinced me. His explanation of what the surgery would accomplish was brief. I had already decided to trust him based on his reputation as a doctor. Having made that original decision, I was highly motivated to take his advice—even if it was costly and inconvenient.

If you don't get anything else out of this entire book, please take this idea with you. If you want to make more sales, faster, and in greater amounts than you ever thought possible, you need to focus a great deal of time, resources, and energy on creating and positioning yourself as the expert and authority in your field.

When you have authority...

- People expect to have a successful encounter (this is a big one!)

- People listen to what you have to say

- People expect to pay more

- People look forward to meeting you

- People trust your suggestions

- People want to spread the word about what you're doing

- ...and much more!

This subject is so important that I can't possibly begin to do it justice by writing one chapter on it. I will write a book on this subject specifically in the future, but for now, just know that your focus should always be on positioning yourself as the authority in your marketplace. This is the only way to truly dominate in the selling environment with realative ease. This concept is something that I focus on in great depth when I'm working with my coaching clients. If you would like to discuss ways that I can help you create and position yourself as an authority in your marketplace, feel free to email me at Rodney@MarketingSS.com or you can contact me at 770.847.6611. This is a concept that can dramatically change your business and lifestyle!

CHAPTER 8

This System Is Your MAGIC PILL for Dominating Your Marketplace

The concepts that you've heard above may sound a bit daunting. You're being told to achieve dominance through confidence, psychology, and a whole lot of elbow grease. Meanwhile, you're up against competitors who can reach thousands or hundreds of thousands of people a day with one TV ad. You must be thinking… "There's no way you can match that." "Can you really hope to compete with a super-sized ad budget?

Well, yes and no. Your long-term goals should include attaining the kind of budget that lets you afford a first-rate advertising campaign—and your current marketing efforts should support that. When it comes to dominating your sales market, I always tell entrepreneurs, managers, and sales professionals "If you do not or your company does not have at least $1,000,000 of liquid cash sitting around that can be invested in advertising and marketing campaigns, you must be willing to put forth a lot of sweat equity to reach your potential clients. And you must have a system in place that will allow you to further develop those relationships until you're in a position to consistently invest large sums of money in persuading the masses to do business with you."

When I make this statement, people tend to look at me like I'm being totally ridiculous. Most of my clients aren't currently investing heavily in advertising or marketing. You probably aren't, either. You may be thinking to yourself, "$1,000,000 seems a little ambitious." Even if you're highly motivated to increase your revenue, you may imagine doubling or tripling your client base, but you probably haven't considered that you need to keep increasing your client base until you reach this level of assets. But I assure you, this figure is actually very conservative; especially if you're in a large market and you want to consistently market for the entire year!

Let's take a look at an average budget range you would need to consistently advertise and market through traditional media, during peak times of the day, with high-quality production and messaging for an entire year in a mid-sized market:

Billboards: $80,000 – $840,000
Radio: $100,000 – $960,000
Television: $150,000 – $1,000,000

The estimates above are based on the approximate amount of money that would be needed to have a consistent campaign that is powerful enough to constantly bring in a slew of clients that are ready to do business with you over the course of a 12-month time frame. If you have this kind of money lying around, then you're in a position to be creative and focus on working smart to dominate your marketplace. You don't need extraordinary elbow grease or a gift for wooing new prospects over the phone. You can afford to worry about which spokesperson would best align with your core values, and how many times a day to post to your corporate Twitter account. But if you're like most people reading this book, you don't have this kind of marketing capital just lying around! If that's you, it does not take a rocket scientist to realize that you must be willing to work your ass off and also work super smart in order to have a chance at dominating your marketplace consistently.

Most businesses are like yours: They're not Coca-Cola or Apple, and they can't reach millions of people by putting a talking animal in their ads. But you have an advantage over your small and medium-sized business competitors. If you're willing to put the principles from this book into action, you have the tools you need to keep expanding and keep consistently bringing in more customers and more revenue. The good news is that it can be accomplished... you just have to have the right mindset and the right system in place to help you dominate. You may be small for now, but your attitude and strategic ability will be those of a Fortune 500 company. We've seen the strategies that will take you there; now let's look at how they work together to help you compete with the top businesses in your field.

SALES GENERATION SYSTEM

Earlier in this book, I taught you about the number one challenge in business: obscurity. Overcoming obscurity is the key to totally dominating your market. You must have a system in place that will allow you to thoroughly address the three levels of obscurity. Do this, and you'll have a system that allows you to mimic (on a smaller scale) the effect that big businesses have on the marketplace due to their ginormous advertising and marketing budget.

First, figure out how most existing clients are hearing about you, and build on that. Focus on low-cost methods of gaining publicity like sponsored events, social media campaigns and word-of-mouth referrals. Establish a system to consistently bring in new customers by cold calling. Next, demonstrate your value by creating pitches that are focused on the client's interests, and continually fine-tuning them based on what works and doesn't work. Create ads that actually tell clients why they need you. And when it comes to your website, consider adding informative content that will encourage visitors to stay longer. Only when you have executed all these steps, and created a large base of clients that know about you and your brand, should you focus on making your brand ubiquitous.

Many small businesses don't understand this. Oftentimes they end up burning through lots of cash because they try to compete in the big business realm, but don't have pockets that are deep enough to constantly promote like a big business. They don't understand the ultimate strategy behind their advertisements. Try to create a viral advertising icon like the Geico Gecko when you have one thousandth of Geico's budget, and you'll fail. This is guaranteed!

Start paying attention to the difference between how big businesses design an advertising campaign and how small businesses design an advertising campaign using the same media platforms, and you will notice a distinct difference in the use of the platform. Big businesses typically use these media outlets for brand awareness so they can stay on the top level of the client's mind, while small businesses typically try to use these traditional platforms to directly sell. Unfortunately, when you try to use these traditional media for directly selling your product or service, it rarely provides the desired effect.

If your advertising budget was big enough, you could use these platforms to position yourself as the top dog or only dog in your market for what you offer, but if you don't have the budget, you end up reaching a lot of people but not using the proper strategy to get people comfortable with your product or services. Your prospective client hasn't heard of you before, and so a single message doesn't complete the process of convincing them that they should buy. Your client doesn't see you as a well-known name, so they won't consider you as the default option, no matter how prestigious the advertising venue. You should aim to target the same people multiple times—even if it's a much smaller number of people. And you should use direct methods of communication, like phone calls, that let you actually explain why your product is worthwhile.

If you have the money to play the traditional media game effectively, then you just need to focus on maximizing your strategy so you get the biggest return on investment. If you don't have the money to play the traditional media game the right way, then you need to have a system in place that will allow you to do five key things:

1. Find affordable ways to contact large sums of people who may be interested in what you do or offer.

2. Have an irresistible offer in place that causes people who might be predisposed to take advantage of your product or service to lean forward.

3. Have a way to capture their contact information so you can build a database.

4. Have a process in place that persuades them to take advantage of an immediate offer. Scheduling a consultation, installation, or new subscription should be seamless from their perspective.

5. Have a process in place that allows you to easily build a long-term valuable relationship with your database of new friends.

Design a plan that lets you contact clients regularly (but not too frequently) with news and offers, give updates via social media to those who are interested, and give quick feedback to clients who have questions or complaints.

The system listed above can work for any entrepreneur, manager, or sales professional. This system puts you in a position of power because it allows you to control the relationship with the end user. When you advertise in traditional media, it is typically very expensive because the media owns the relationship with the end users, but this approach will allow you to significantly cut out the middleman and start building an asset.

Here's how this might work in practice. Let's say that you own a bakery that you've had for the last ten years. Up to that point, you just focused on traditional forms of advertising to generate business.

You're spending money on newspaper ads and flyers for each new client you get. This may work, but it doesn't get any easier or cheaper over time—no matter how many clients you already have, each ad brings in the same number of new clients. You're paying a premium for new customers, and you're competing against every other bakery that decides to put out an ad.

Now let's say you decide to set up a sales generation system for your business based on the strategies in this book. Now your primary focus revolves around establishing authority, generating value and overcoming obscurity. Now your main strategies are low-cost methods:

- cold calling (selling your baked goods to other businesses like coffee shops)

- word of mouth (clever strategies like offering clients discounts on gift cards)

- low-volume but highly effective marketing (ads that show why you're the best name in town when it comes to wedding cakes).

As a result, over the next four years, you end up creating a relationship with over 10,000 people within your market. They know who you are, and you have their contact information. You could send out one email to your list of friends offering a one-day-only deal on cupcakes. If even one percent of your mailing list takes you up on the deal, and each spends $20 on cupcakes, you've generated $2000 worth of extra sales within 24 hours. How awesome is that? Pretty awesome! You've gone from expending tons of time and energy in recruiting new business to doing so with virtually no effort. Looked at another way, with your old technique you were expanding your business arithmetically—adding the same number of dollars to your revenue stream each week or month. Now you're expanding geometrically— potentially multiplying your income with each action you take.

The sales generation system can allow you to do that if you're willing to consistently focus on executing the system. Sure, you'll start out gaining clients painstakingly one by one. But the gains you make will be fast, effective and long-lasting because your clients know you, trust you and are delighted to have a business relationship with you.

This system can also work if you don't own your own business. Imagine that you're a car sales professional, and you decided to set up a sales generation system. You refine your pitch to take each potential buyer through the five stages of sales, and you focus on projecting authority. You decide to track each customer interaction after it's over to record what the outcome was, and to spend some time each Friday looking over your progress from the preceding week. You track what concepts and arguments work best to win over potential buyers so your sales will continuously increase. Over the next three years, you focus intensively on executing this system. A result, you end up establishing a relationship with over 4000 people in your market who know you, like you, and trust you because you've been executing the system.

If your work on commission, that's great! If not, your performance may win you a raise or promotion. But sometimes employees find themselves victim to the whims of the marketplace. These types of sales skills will still help you in a tight job market. Let's say that the car lot you're working for decides to shut down. The average salesperson would be in a very difficult position because they would have to start from scratch again. You would be in a position of power, because you have an asset that will allow you to easily find another job at another car lot. You can simply point to your sales record as a reason to hire you—and if car lots aren't hiring, you can market your skills to any other business that requires selling skills! The product you're selling is yourself, and you can dominate the market with a proven track record. In the worst-case scenario, you're still good because you have an asset in place that you can find creative ways to monetize if you need to.

We've seen how a smart approach to selling can help you quickly position yourself as an authority in your market, save money on expensive advertising campaigns over the long term, and provide you with an asset that you can use to generate thousands (possibly millions) of dollars over the length of your career. I'd love to hear your feedback on how this system worked for you! Not sure about the next steps to take? I'm available for one-on-one coaching to develop a Sales Generation System specifically tailored to your business. I'll learn about your specific needs and challenges, and create a step-by-step blueprint that will put you on the fast track to market domination. With one of my customized systems, you'll have fast answers to answer tricky questions like:

- How do I set an advertising budget?

- How do I know if my cold call pitch is as effective as it could be?

- Which of my ads are effective, and which are a waste of money?

If you would like to discuss setting up a Sales Generation System for your business, call 770.847.6611 or email me directly at Rodney@MarketingSS.com.

www.ingramcontent.com/pod-product-compliance
Lightning Source LLC
Chambersburg PA
CBHW060324220326
41598CB00027B/4412